I BLEED THROUGH THIS INK

There's passion in your purpose

by

Piere Ingram

I Bleed Through This Ink takes the reader on a spiritually-driven journey of personal transformation, self-reflection, overcoming obstacles, and everything in between. Through heartfelt and soulful poetic storytelling from beginning to end, Piere invites one to grow and heal, even in the face of untold hardship. Moreover, this poignant collection of poetry serves as a reminder of embracing one's God-given gifts and the Lord's sacred guidance along their path to greatness. By book's end, the reader will have undergone an undeniable metamorphosis that inspires them to see God's divine light in all things.

CONTENTS

PICK THE PEN UP

I write till I fall asleep

I wake up to pick my pen up

And then I started writing again

About what it took to help me start writing again

Then I faded into this paper I was writing on

My soul was expressed on every line

Every line was a detail of what I was going through

Through these details, the audience started to live my life

This life that I was living inside was pointed to you

I was headed to Jesus Christ

Pick your pen up

My pen is carrying up my cross

CONTINUE WITH
THE JOURNEY

I know you have heard this before

How I was sidetracked and detoured

But this time I am going to get my life straight

I am going on a trip to the shore

The way that I picked for myself fooled me once again

Stop playing tricks with my mind

We're not going through this again

I continued this continuous journey

Giving God the fight

I couldn't see anything

I was blinded by what was good

I couldn't see what was right

In front of me, I say once again

Here on this continuous journey to win

IF IT WAS EASY EVERYBODY WOULD BE DOING IT

I'm moving this movement

If it was easy everybody would be doing it

I'm moving it into position to speak

My spirit on paper

I have a lot of people to reach

Shut down the hype; I'm in position

This man is right and lead by the Holy Spirit

While everybody else is asleep I am
up writing through the storm

The lightning strikes the page

And every word I write with thunder

I like the light

Y'all been warned,

And it's been proven that if it was easy,
everybody would be doing it

PERFECT PICTURES

Picture a perfect picture

That was imperfect inside of this frame

Picture a imperfect picture

Inside of this one clouded frame

Picture a picture that was perfect

Then it will be nothing to fix

Picture what God thought of you
when he created all of this

When I say this, I mean you

This is my point of view

I know how you see yourself

He sees you, as you

You don't need to be anybody else

Perfect pictures

Piere Ingram

A SENSE OF URGENCY

I won't wait

Who knows what tomorrow has for me

I have to do this now

Who knows what now can turn into

The rain doesn't wait to fall

And death doesn't wait for you to come

No hesitating for a minute

I have to get this done

Why I say now, let me tell you

Minutes turn into hours to derail you

Time on earth is man-made

Life is just a minute

You waited too long now you feel betrayed

Sense of urgency

JESUS

Jewels in my heart

Everlasting love

That lasts forever

that could never ever tear us apart

Stand up for what you believe in

Unity is what brought us together

In you, we are always together

Saw what we never saw

'Cause you were with him from day one

Jesus

YOU POET

Just a regular guy

With a gift

That gift was his light

That poet started to write

You poet out on paper

What was created out of that

A book about his life

He had to write many nights

You poet out of his heart

He wrote himself out of the dark

All he needed was a little spark

And that was that

It caught on to many things

It began to become ablaze

But you poet wasn't amazed

Like the others that wouldn't listen

They heard what got him to this position

But never really knew what he been through

They only saw the results

After the fact

And a matter of fact

After that, you poet

Was known all over the map

CHAPTER 1

This is just the beginning; I can feel
it in every cell of my body

There is so much more to learn

These words I speak comes from a place of peace

Love and above everything else I have ever imagined.

I saw myself.

This buzz I once had made me forget myself

But I had the courage to stand up to everyone else.

I was so beside myself.

Chapter 1

Everything you do should start with the man in the mirror

If I could stand up to him that's where we win

Say goodbye to sin

Now I know my identity in Christ

By living my life through him

Chapter 1

For all the things I've done is washed away
by accepting him as God's son

Chapter 1

Piere has died to this world

He lives through the father and son

He has a new chapter

They live as one

It is done

Chapter 1

SPIRITUAL GIFTS

These encouraging gifts from the spirit walk
with me, talks with me, it's part of me

I never again want to lose a part of me
by not using my spiritual gifts

To inspire others and lift them when
they feel they have no purpose

I'm just touching the surface

On this line I write

I'm fine, I'm light

As you can see I'm bright

God gave me this pen to write out this plan for life

He planned it right together with him

Everything feels right on time with him
and never feels out of place

He put me right in place

Right where I need to be to use my spiritual gifts

TIME ZONE

I've lost track of time

My mind finds time to travel where I never asked it to go

But it seems to have a mind of its own

Lost in this time zone

The hour glass is broken

From past moments

Taken over my thoughts

I thought this would be easy

But it seems to be not like I expected

Now I feel neglected

And out of choices

My choices are void as I chase down time

Like I'm going to really catch up to it and
pull it back where I want it to be

See I grab on the hands of time like it's a tug of war

And the hands were a rope

But nope, I should have used my time wisely

But I was too busy doing dope

The slope was very slippery

I tried climbing back up

And I did it with God's help

All this time in God's time zone

And I only failed because I tried to do it on my own

Time Zone

HOUR GLASS

Time is temporary

It tempts me not to believe it

But I see it past at the same time

A flashback enters my mind

A fast track leaves behind what I saw in the hour glass

Upside down the hours went

Give me another chance to start over again so I can vent

God sent me a sign in the minutes of time

Created in this hour glass

The sand camouflage the genie
bottle turned upside down

Gave me permission to take off on this magic carpet

Towards my future regardless of my past

Thank you, Lord, for more than just this hour glass

BEFORE MY TIME

It was planned before my time

These seeds were planted on every line I wrote

It started to grow

I started to know

Before my time

I saw this vision painted inside of my mind

So I painted these words on every single line

Before my time

I started to watch what God's hands
do inside of this clock

His short hand was on my life

While internally his long hand created things
in the kingdom for me to watch

Everything I saw I wrote

It began to get cold

I put on my coat

I guess through all that, seasons change before my time

Before my time where kingdoms reign

For eternity, I'm learning me

When I read his word I fly high as an eagle

The kingdoms bird

Before my time

WHATEVER SUITS YOU

Love who you want to love, whatever suits you

Your world changes inside of you

Do what you love, you'll be placed inside yourself

There's no one else better than you

Love whatever suits you

Put your suit on of God's love

You'll walk out the door with confidence

This confidence wore a suit of compassion

It will drive you to love yourself even better

Whatever suits you

CLEAN

For years you've been dirty

It's like you've been eating with pigs

I know you're just trying to live

You just want to be clean

From all this mess in the world

Just ask God to clean you up

He will wash your face and wash your hands

But you kept walking in dirt

The typical man

So, Jesus washed your feet

No longer were you walking in dirt

You're clean

AWARENESS IS KEY

Awareness is key to transformation

When I stopped doing drugs I began to
be aware of the sickness in my head

After I began to become aware I started to notice

I was addicted to self-limiting emotional states

I was addicted to the old me

I know you're wondering what I mean by 'the old me?'

I mean a person that beat himself about everything

He did instead of forgiving himself

You that are reading this

Awareness is key

WEAKNESS

A day turns into a week

Where did my days go?

Why do I feel so weak?

My strength is found in God's Word

Why don't I read his Word that lives in me?

I ask myself then a whisper I hear

A whisper I hear, speak

I feel love when I hear it

My spirit loves me back

Wouldn't want it any other way than that

In my weakness is strength

I am created through Jesus

I'm loving my weakness

Piere Ingram

LET YOUR DREAMS
CARRY YOU

Many sleepless nights taking action on your dreams

Sleepless nights in Seattle

Isn't always what it seems

I saw the dreams starting to carry you

When you felt like you had no more to offer

You said no more; don't even bother

Don't get bored; you have a purpose

Your purpose is to read what I write

To get yourself out of the darkness; to share the light

You see what was gifted in me

On my journey, I started doubting myself

See I'm just like you in some ways

I let you know what's going on in my mind

What do you think of the view?

I wrote this to let your dreams carry you

MY PEN MOVES ME

I'm so connected to my dream

My pen moves me when I'm asleep

When you read this you are going
to be saying to yourself

This is deep

I can hear you now

Your hands moving in silence and
you can't put the book down

Every word you read change the dreams in your head

And what you knew about your life

My life had connected you instead

You hear the words in my head

How excited do you get when you
move to a new realm of thinking

Asking yourself why haven't you been
thinking this deep all along

Come on now, my pen moves you

What did you think it would do?

Read this from a beautiful view

Have you ever been here before?

Have you ever traveled before to a place in your soul?

Then you definitely know why my pen moves you

BYE BYE

I'll be back when you're ready for this

Wait, what?

Well, let me tell you now since you really want to know

I want to tell you something that will show

That you probably already know

You just ignored it like it didn't exist

Now you want to know what really existed

How dare you risk it

Telling yourself what you know inside

Before you believed someone else

I had to save you from yourself

You would have taken what you knew
and destroyed everyone else

Bye bye

Piere Ingram

A DIAMOND IS MADE
UNDER PRESSURE

Pressure is a gift to make you better

Better is what we get when we don't stop

He tells me to tell you a lot

I know something about you

Yeah you

That's reading this right now

Step out of the crowd

Come by yourself because you're
leaving the same way you came

So stop worrying about feeling ashamed

He just wants to show us the way

To save us from ourselves

A series of thoughts that want to walk with the world

He wants to use us in a mighty way

I bleed through this ink

But we have to give up the world

I know you're tired of being confused

And you're feeling abused

The Lord is amused with your plans for the next day

Stop walking by yourself like you own
the key to your own way

He is the door, plus the key, and the doorway

REFLECTION

I look in this mirror

I see a soul that has been touched by an angel

That angel was mom as I think about
the times we spent together

These are the things I think about
when I see my reflection

This section of my brain where memories lie

I try to reflect on the good

To get past these moments when I start missing you

I see you, dad, when I look through these crystal balls

I'm in this for the long hall

So many things you taught me too that
determined my next step to victory

These memories will live on through my reflection

I see so much now even more than
before even though you're gone

Are you really is the question because every
time I see me I see your reflection

I think I'll go take a rest with peace in my soul

TEN DAYS IN

These constant memories of things that don't serve me

I'm just ten days' in

These days of me feeling I'm not worthy

But feeling worried

I'm just ten days' in

From the truth, I'm trying to survive

I'm just ten days in loving this natural high

The sweat combined with these tears

Leaves a pool of memories that flooded
these bad memories out

I'm just ten days' in

I'm just now finding out what this is about

I shout with tears of happiness running down my face

I'm ten days in without leaving a
trace from where I have been

It's almost washed away because I've been
walking through the pain as it rains

I'm just ten days' in

I think about these ten days as they pass my way

Father loves the water

I think about him through my ten days in
then I felt the wind blow against my skin

I thought about giving up in these ten days

Then I think about how far I have gained

This pain never matched up to how far I came in the rain

I don't want to risk it

Going back now

Ten days backwards doesn't look familiar to me

But I see these ten days is turning out to be the
best times of my life and I'm just ten days in

WHAT ABOUT TOMORROW

What about tomorrow?

I just know today as I see it

Just be it.

Be what...

Be what God called you to be

See you watching but you just don't believe it

That's what's really going on with you...

You just can't believe it

I believe it and I see it so what about tomorrow

If tomorrow never comes what have you done today?

To see it, you have to believe it

Believe who you truly are or who you were destined to be

See, walk without sight

The shiny objects are bright and it
seems to be blinding your sight

This isn't right

What about tomorrow if today you don't get it right

Piere Ingram

A WONDERFUL PLACE TO BE

I'm stuck in this moment beautifully made by God

A wonderful place to be laying in his arms

He covered me up when the world attacks

He picked me up when I fell on my back

I owe my father never to look back

Back up, look at where you came from

Where are you now?

As a matter of fact

I'm back

In this wonderful place to be

I can see through the spirit of what
God made through me

WRITE OUT OF PAIN

This came right out of pain

I've endured this game

This gave me a way to write out my pain

It had to go somewhere

So tired of having these things stuck in my head

So I write out my pain

So much to gain

So much healing power for many to see

This masterpiece, that was created through me

What is there to gain?

Don't answer that, let me write out my pain

I'm so relieved

From the release of false reality that dwelled inside

If you're not ready now, get ready for this ride

As I write out my pain

Ashamed of who I once was

So now I can tell you who I was with no holding back.

I came to write out my pain, and that's that

Piere Ingram

BRIGHT PATH

I see everything clearly now as I
look forward to the reward

At the end of the road a bright path
I see as the story is told

I tell the story to my audience on Facebook

How I got out of the abuse

And if you abuse yourself, you can get out of it too

Let me open up my mouth and tell you

Don't let your past come up and derail you

I know the tunnel is dark and you can't see a thing

But we carry the light for we can see
beautiful things in dark places

We are just human beings

But we walk out with God's spirit

What is near it?

I say the throne; I tell you

We don't have to do it on our own

Even when stones are being thrown

This bright path

POWER

Power is in the Word of God

Power is in you when you are weak

It shows, we know the power in you

Because of the words you speak

Your words give me goosebumps

They are so deep

Peep what I found in me

It really excited me to visit me more

More of me is what I found alone

Alone in this place to roam

And Rome wasn't built in a day

So I stayed in this place to play

For a long time searching but I finally found my way

I played around, didn't take it serious

Until a part of me died when I died period

I finally got it straight

Now I can face my fears

I've been traveling to find this place in my mind for years

Power

Piere Ingram

A DAY IN MY SHOES

I woke up this morning with a lot on my mind

I knew I forgot to write last night

So last night is what I woke up to

And last night was a constant fight

That's some real stuff to wake up to do, you agree?

When you can't find the perfect things to write

These obstacles start to blind your sight

Then you start holding on to things that don't serve you

Now you can't see a thing and these
things are what define you

A Day in my shoes

I SAW NATIONS IN YOUR EYES

Look in the mirror, I know you see your eyes

But I see nations, this is no surprise

See the uprising of your faith

You jump up because of the takeover

Saying, "I don't know what came over me"

Suddenly you began to walk into your destiny

You felt like the darkness tried to shame you

But the same God that made you overcame you

He picked you over what you thought of yourself

If you couldn't be you, then you'll be someone else

That's a great mistake and you are no mistake

You stand by heaven's gate

I saw nations in your eyes

WHAT CAN YOU DO

Ask yourself

You do need help

I won't let the pride destroy you this time

You have to do it this time

I know you've got a lot by walking
into things you've never seen

Before you know it, you'll become free

You love to be free

It feels good doesn't it

I know the world feels; F*** your feelings

You can hear the world talking to
you with this familiar voice

Telling you to keep the faith

And trust the process

Not the man with the corrupt objects

That he's created in the dark mind
of his to blow up the world

But still, you believe this man with a hardened heart

The darkness is ready to tear this world apart

What can you do?

YOU WALKED

You crawled, then you walked

You stuttered, then you talked

You didn't believe, then you saw

Who could this be if it wasn't me

You know this was the Holy Spirit because
you moved without a single thought

You knew this was smart

You knew this was wisdom and you being connected

God's spirit, can you hear it?

Shhh

Be quiet, I can

And then miracles started to happen
in your transformation

It was the transformation of your
mind, rewind, what happened

Piere Ingram

It's time to be refined through your passion

Just to write this single line

Fine, let's walk

I'm ready

What better time than now?

It's the why that pushes me

You don't need to know the how

Wow! You just walked

Wow! You just talked

Do you believe the things that God does through you?

SECRETS

These secrets that were hidden were brought to the light

They couldn't put up a fight to hide it

The violence was exposed to the light

The violent moments in secret was hiding in the dark

Thought it would never be seen until
that love started to spark

That's just part of the secrets in the dark places

Hoping to never to be seen

The scene was camouflaged if you know what I mean

If you do please speak up

It's the voices that are hidden that
can do wonderful things

It's so beautiful when God hid this in human beings

Seeing things that would be in your world as secrets

This life exposes all secrets

Piere Ingram

JUST THIS ONE TIME

It's what you say to yourself before the
consequences started to happen

Just this one time

Do you get caught in this vicious cycle?

Of one timer many times over

I'm so over this one-time stuff

Just this one time I hear in my head

Head over to the time clock now and punch out

From repeating this insanity

Do you hear me playing my part to the symphony?

No more one-time stuff

MESSAGES OF ABUNDANCE

Open the gateway to abundance

Let the message flow

Let's grow

Dance to the message of freedom

Can you hear it so clearly?

It kills all the fear

No more looking out the rear mirror of fear

God steers me

While the world stares at me

These stairs I walk up leads me to him

I follow the message of abundance

This old me is redundant to what this new me is doing

All while I am dancing to these messages of abundance

Messages of abundance

THE KINGDOM LIFE

My heart is treasure-filled with faith

Thank you, Lord, for your grace

Can you see the kingdom lifestyle
written all over my face?

We walk with integrity with the liberty of the Lord

Statues are broken

We stay faithful to the one true king of everything

Bring forth truth like you always have

The same truth that brought us
through our past mistakes

Putting in the work like this is your last chance

This is where we advance

And watch the kingdom take its place

Where we all get the crown

Because we held our faith through
all the pain on solid ground

Life in the kingdom is what I imagine

Until he comes back

Not concerned with this world and what it does

All that it speaks is no part of me

It's crooked

Look at it

What has been made

VIVID PICTURES

Do you see these vivid pictures, like I do?

Places I've never thought I would be

But they are so real

So real, it feels like I've been here before

I go forth and live out these imaginations

In my dreams of real repeated action steps

Moving forth diligently in the presence of God's love

Oh sweet vivid pictures

Painted by words, I see the scriptures

Painting God's vision of me

These creations of pictures diversify

Who am I to criticize?

These vivid pictures of me.

FAILING FORWARD

Don't be afraid to fail forward, now, don't wait

So what, you made a mistake

Learn that lesson

The lesson is your weapon

Stay locked and loaded

For what was chosen for you

The quicker you fail, the faster you win

So what you failed

Try it again

You'll be wiser next time

You know the saying, "What goes up, must come down"

But the growth is the lesson on the way down

Jesus is the foundation, built on solid ground

God's Word is so profound

That's where I found myself

Again, thank you for letting me fail forward.

THIS IS SO AMAZING

What you do to me is so amazing

This beam of light you tattooed in my soul

Can never be covered up at all

Even when I fall

'Cause I will stand up again

With this beam of light, it never dimmed

Even when I fail, because Love never fails

In the darkest of hours, there is power in Love

When you love yourself differently, the inner

perspectives start to show

This is so amazing

This love inside of you

 I feel in every breath

I take it that You still love me

Even when I make mistakes

I never give up believing in love

It is so real

I can still feel it

I drop to my knees

To worship Your Love

This is so amazing

TEMPERATURE

Lukewarm soul

Sometimes hot

The rest follows the flock.

I feel around for the right temperature

But somehow, I am stuck in my mental block

Flow state controls time

Steady rolling around in my own mind

Premature thoughts expand on a new

lifeline

It's pumping for mass exposure

But only to my disclosure

It happened in God's time

Confined to Thee

It would be

For those that could see

Keep it to the right temperature.

Temperature

DARK MOMENTS

Dark moments in this light area of my brain

abstracted from my soul

My heart is warm from the world being so cold

Raised from feeling so low

But when I reach this peak of my highs, I arose

Unstoppable to any type of attack

I spoke up loudly to drown out the voices

Transformed from my addictions of feeling

every thought that woke up inside these dark moments

These spirits of light talking in God's whisper

I hear

I follow the trail to victory

I am set free from this flesh

I live more diligently

With no worries about tomorrow

Turning these dark moments into my light

Giving the fight to God

I am unstoppable in these dark moments.

IN MY WORLD

There's full of love

The dove flies above the hate

If I make a mistake

Say something

Help me fix this wrong

I'll become the best version of me

Let me enjoy my flight

There's peace in the air

I dare you to be different

Welcome to my world

where words are life

These words came true while spoken

Every letter is my light

Every time I speak, they come to life

You want them?

You'll have to pay the price

Imagine my world

AS I WALK THROUGH DEEP THOUGHT

As I walked through deep thought

Words spin through my mind

I find a safe haven

Through spoken word

Have you heard?

I'm building from the dirt

Even when my feelings get hurt

God created every single thought

As I walk through deep thought

STRUGGLE INSIDE MINDS EYE

This struggle inside my mind's eye

Revises of a plan to take me out

Self-doubt, what is this about?

I control my destiny

I'm moved by the Holy Spirit

Do you hear it?

Hear what?

Your mind says your spirit is talking to you

You're not listening

Moved by your flesh,

Put that to rest

This is a mess

Messenger of peace

Let the message be released

Don't let it feast on your mind

Find out what it's about

Don't drown it out

Dreams running about

Mind conditioned to doubt

You got this

Stop this

You finally found out what this is about

Struggle inside my mind's eye

MY GOD

My God is bigger than circumstances

I've advanced my faith from belief

Love for one another

My God is bigger

than how I feel

I'll kill my flesh

to become my best

My God is bigger than death

Through death, we live

Let's give it all we got

I will not give up

He never gave up on us

Until the day we turn into dust

I praise

Our God is bigger

My God

OH THE PRESSURE

All this pressure

I felt when I was a kid

Needed to write a list

I felt like nothing,

I tried to slit my wrist

Wanted to give my thoughts a rest

Flashbacks haunting me

Oh the pressure beating on my flesh

These suicidal thoughts were watching me when I write

An ongoing sickness and I couldn't put up a fight

You can be my witness

You saw this when I write

The darkness tried to shine over the light

But I write

To give more than me, the light

I'm steady writing while I am high as a kite

ONE CHANCE

Hurry Hurry

911 Ambulance

One Life

One Chance

One Symphony

One Dance

I did it now

Who's in the crowd?

Too tall to bow

But I did get on my knees

Oh God, hold me

I don't know me

I boldly go where no writer has gone before

Inside of Jesus' heart

I have reached the core

These sores are healed

If you had sores before and they were healed

Then my God is real

One chance

QUIET TIME

It once was so loud inside

There was nowhere to hide

Jesus arrived

I was no longer deprived

This quiet time with him

Jesus held my hand

I was no longer corrupted by man

My knees were on solid ground

Shhhh

Quiet time a whispered sound

So profound

This emptiness I once felt disappeared

In your grace, I've tasted the bread of life

Love was written on my face

Just a touch of grace will change your whole life

Imagine this inside of your mind

Take his hand for quiet time.

POWERFUL WORDS

As I contemplate my thoughts

These words want to move without me

Powerful words that reroute me

to my own world

of new things to come

Powerful words under the sun

It feels good to sit under the shade

while my old life passes away

I walk, I look around

My powerful words sometimes have me down

I told myself the truth

Oh do I wish my feelings were bulletproof.

HEART BEHIND MY EYES

My heart is crying out for help

It beats for some type of relief

I know I can see it

This is real

I believe it

Heart behind my eyes

I realize this pain

Heart pumps the blood through my heart

This is a start to a great friendship

Heart behind my eyes

I can see the truth in your eyes

I can hear it beat the tears that fall down my cheek

Give your heart some relief

This truth I feel it and see it; I can't conceal it

My heart behind my eyes poured out like acrylic

Heart behind my eyes.

CHAINS

Break the chains, be free and humble

Cross over the clouds, watch your feet; don't stumble

Heavens in your heart, I feel it

With every chance, hold your hands out

Patch the avalanche

Tears fall forever

Don't fear the last dance

Chains wrapped around brains

Kind of strange they all are in a trance

Wake up! Wake up! they're stuck in this world

with chains wrapped around their ankles.

PAINTED WORDS

I pick up the brush, I'm ready to paint

Let me paint a picture for you of
this fire that grows inside

I walk in truth painted in words

A whispered thought painted in
thirds in every letter I bought

Filling the curves, curving around the
feelings I am feeling for you

Let my painted words describe what I am willing to do

Painted words.

A LIFE TO LIVE

Live the life you want to live

Forget, forgive

Just live the life you want to live

This life is what you make it

Make it a good one, I say

I pray for it

A life to give more than just to self

To live a life, to give your life to Jesus Christ is a life to live

There is more than what you see

We can't see the wind

We know it's there

We feel He cares in every word

The Living Word

He created the flight that lives in birds

So, imagine what He has created inside of you

This is what sets us free

A caged-in bird, set free through poetry

A life to live.

NO MORE WORRIES

It always hurt to see you cry

I used to come into your room and wonder why

I was too young to understand

How these feelings bounce off walls like rubber bands

I would duck, wonder, and hide under the covers

No more worries

Here today, gone tomorrow

I'm just glad there's no more sorrow

I follow the love that came from this deepest pain

This love in this picture frame

TORN APART

Amen! I'm coming together from being torn apart

The heart

The start to this mess

Another test

A testimony leaves my flesh

To be the testimony

My flesh is lonely

Really, is that the most important
part of what got torn apart

No, it wasn't so; I had to write about it

God has fixed me up

No reason for me to doubt it

Tell the truth of how I got rerouted

A new journey of soul searching

Finally found it

Thank you, Lord, from the heart

Regaining my strength from being torn apart

WRITING IN THE MIDDLE OF THIS TORNADO

As this world speeds

I write in the middle of this tornado

I see my mind spin

Then I follow through with the vision

This mission that flows, grows through this pain

The light found on this flight

I'm gone; come on, find me; I'm relaxed with God

Everything about this is right

When I write, I see you, mom,

I feel you dad

I touch places that are not seen with the human eye

Please take a walk with me

While I write in the middle of this tornado

A BLACK DOCTOR SEUSS

I know it's not my color

One would have to wonder

No one could drag me under

Stop rhyming man, damn!

This is what I do

If I didn't, I would be you

On the other hand

I am a man that can take it, and
make it into something deep

I take leaps off the page

Travel through my mind

I'm back to paper again

Then relax

Let my soul take over

I'm back to writing again

JUST KEEP SHARING
THE LOVE

The pretty blue bird

The pretty dove

My loving heart keeps sharing the love

I live from my heart

With His love, there's nothing that can tear us apart

This is just the start

A beautiful friendship to a beautiful friendship

A targeted dart

aimed at what's real

I can feel it

I can't conceal it

The love that God gives to us is unbreakable

Even when we break

This is no mistake

We break to be put together again

Better than ever before

The core to a solid foundation

The Word that holds all truth

The flesh holds no standing to the spirit

The light shines

I thank you, God, for keep sharing the love

THOSE LAST DAYS

Those conversations we would have with no one around

The nights we spent on our knees praying together

Those were the last days

I appreciate every moment we spent

Give me this time to vent

Those long talks at night were heaven sent

What I would do for those nights again

These are the things I think about

When I write about these last days

Your wisdom erased all my fears

When I think about our fights, our tears

If I really dig deep, those last days were thirty-six years

Piere Ingram

SERVANT'S HEART

There's passion in my purpose

This purpose hit the surface

These serpents attack

It's how we respond or is it how we react

Massive attack on our souls

Be bold or fold

There's no in-between

Either you're hot or you're cold

Finish upon your road

It's a fight for our souls

Don't believe what you've been told

There's a price to be paid

Guess what?

Jesus has already paid the toll

So there's no reason why you should fold

Stand tall no matter what

There are no doors that are shut

These possibilities are endless

Be relentless even if in a rut

In God we trust

A servant's heart

I SPEAK THROUGH
THIS HEARTBEAT

Never take life for granted

At any minute this life can vanish

I speak through this heartbeat

Words of transparency

Touch others by example

This testimony speaks through this heartbeat

Temporary emotions

Should I believe this feeling or not

It will go away in moments

Feel nature move inside me spiritually

Grace ables me to face my fears

It puts me inside my place

True living begins in the heart

Expressions of the heart

Through your heartbeat speaks God's Word

DREAMS IN THE WATER

There's no wondering How, When, or Why

These words my water

If I stop swimming, I will die

I'm a shark in these deep waters

I keep swimming no matter what's going on in my mind

Held the pen, I wrote my story

God gets the glory

I'm going to make him proud

No expectations of a wow from the crowd

As long as God sees me, that's all I need

I believe in His Word

In the beginning, the Word already existed

The Word was with God, and the Word was God

So I believe in my dreams in the water

IT'S POSSIBLE

The possible is never impossible

My positivity roars amid the storm

You created the strong mind inside of this vessel

He created this vessel in love

It is possible to love even if you never knew it

I block out everything just to get to it

With no conditions, this conviction inside of me dies

A star is born

Formed to be a vision of me

Stirs up this ambition in me

Counting my blessings is visibly easy to see

It's possible

HABITS

Habits can kill

Habits are real

Habits can be changed

Habits are kind of strange in a weird way

That habit was a choice

Habits are replaced when you're
dedicated and tired of the same

Habits have a voice

What habits did you choose?

What person did you lose?

Inside of that voice, it doesn't shut up

You have to replace it

Face it

Habits control your soul

Dig deep

Don't fall asleep

Please don't fold

Habits are cold

It had no mercy for the person it had under its control

Habits

DANCING TO THE
SOUND OF SILENCE

You grabbed my hand

I grabbed yours

We started to dance

Emotions enhanced by the silence of every step we take

I feel your breath pressed upon my neck

Guided by the still voice by all due respect

I love this dance we take together,
dancing to the sound of silence

I've missed your presence since you left

Now you're back

Which brought me back because I live through you

Dancing to the sound of silence

EMPATH FRIENDSHIP

This friendship we have is deep

We feel each other's pain until we fall asleep

Imagine stepping into a room drained like a sink

Think about this source of energy
travel to an unknown territory

We share each other's feelings through real stories

Can't change it

So we frame it

How could this be

So we frame it for all to see

How could this be

This empath Friendship

OVERFLOW

Flow over my cup

I need you guys to get a taste

I care about you

Overflow

Lord, please fill me up

I've been empty for a while without you

Why did I ever doubt you

You're the overflow of my cup

This poem is about you

But you already knew about this didn't you?

Silly me to overthink this

I've been looking the wrong way

But still, you filled me up

Overflow

SIMPLE THINGS

It's simple, be you

You'll be someone you never knew

Simple things around you

Things are simple

Things they've never seen

Just be you

Even if they don't understand

Simple things are at hand

If you don't stand for something, you'll fall for anything

Just stick with the simple things

Things are simple if we don't complicate
our thoughts around them.

WILL I SURVIV THROUGH
THE TEST OF TIME

Time is a test

Will you fulfill your purpose at your best?

Or will you just lead with your flesh?

By that time, you see time has been a mess

Listen to the message

Can you hear it?

It can hear you wasting time

Then time uses you internally, you die inside

Please, Lord, give me a chance for
my purpose to be fulfilled

Or can I simply forgive myself for I can be healed?

Then time can be controlled by forming up a plan

Will I survive the test of time?

PLEASE, LORD, TAKE MY HAND.

PAINTED WORDS

I pick up the brush

I'm ready to paint

Let me paint a picture for you of
this fire that grows inside

I walk in truth painted in words

A whispered through painted in
thirds in every letter I bought

Filling the curves, curving around the
feelings I am feeling for you

Let my painted words describe what I am willing to do

Painted Words.

THE GATES ARE OPEN

Come in my friend, be my guest in my home

I am always there when you're feeling alone

Come on in and take a seat where
passion and desire meet.

What do you want to eat?

I did not know. He gave me a book

I opened it up and I took a look

And I love to read, so I ate every word

I enjoyed everything about it

The chapters began to become who I am

"Who am I?" is the question he asked

Then suddenly I remembered I AM.

GRATITUDE

This gratitude changed my attitude
about the things I saw

My gratitude helped me live out the law

This attraction changed the way I was acting

At the age of 12, I started rapping

'cause of the gratitude I have had for the gift

At 16, I made a shift into God's plan
for me to land in His hands

He then brought me to this land of positive things

I just had to search to find this vision of gratitude.

Piere Ingram

HEAR WHAT MY EYES HAD TO SAY

It was one of those days

Where my eyes had many things to say

The day was bright

When she looked in my eyes

They became nightlights in this dark place

My eyes were saying many things

They pointed the way without saying a thing

Hear what my eyes had to say

LIGHT WORK

These words I write are light

Through this twilight, this fight might be light

Once I beat it twice in one night

The fright was too pumped up on what I write.

To hide me but to share myself with the world

I had to be beside myself, just to find myself

To go deep inside myself

I pulled out my soul

And set it right next to me

It told me to write this recipe

In front of me feeling bold

I got tired of the cold

I cuddled with my words

It created a beautiful mold.

A LOT OF P'S!

There's passion in my purpose

Bye Piere

Peace, no negativity

Positive energy

This passive package pushing me through the fight

I play hard to get it right

Played up 'pleased to meet you, Pierre'

Pressure building up to push me

Pleasure pulling me in all directions

Piere's passion pushes him through the pressure

But a diamond was made

Tell me what is better

I wrote my emotions in every letter

Pleased to meet you, too

As you listened, I know you feel my
emotions coasting on paddle boats

The rest goes up in smoke

As I disappear in it

I am a mirror image of what God put in me

So, come and get me and I mean a lot of me

The world's still the same but with a whole lotta P!

Piere Ingram

RAINDROPS

Every tear I shed

Was it in vain?

Every tear that dried up

Once shared my pain

There's no ducking the rain,

I feel it touched my skin

You know where I have been

So, I embraced it,

Face it,

I thought it out to reroute and it
eventually took me to my new life

CHAINS

Break the chains

Be free and humble

Cross over the clouds

Watch your feet, don't stumble

Heavens in your heart

I feel it

With every chance, hold your hands out

Patch the avalanche

Tears fall forever

Don't fear the last dance

Chains wrapped around brains

Kind of strange they are in a trance

Wake up, wake up

They're stuck in this world with chains
wrapped around their ankles

Piere Ingram

FAN THE FLAMES

Arise from the ashes, I came

To fan the flames

I arose chosen

From God to be who I am

Amazingly made for victory

I overcame any challenges I see.

Just what I needed to see

At the moment, this moment in time

This moment was mine

Fan the Flames I came

Out of addiction and fear

This pleasure became my pain

Fearless to this false reality

I see it seems to be not what I believe

Leave from me, demon of shame

Rain to fan the flames.

HEART BEHIND MY EYES

My heart is crying out for help.

It beats for some type of relief I know I can see it

This is real

I believe it

Heart behind my eyes

I realize this pain and hurt pumps
the blood through my heart

This is a start to a great friendship

Heart behind my eyes

I can see the truth in your eyes

I can hear it beat the tears that fall down my cheek

Give your heart some relief

This truth, I feel it

I can't conceal

My heart behind my eyes poured out like acrylic

Heart behind my eyes.

Piere Ingram

THIS IS DEDICATED TO YOU

Piere, you thought you couldn't do this

Look how far you have come

I know you never knew this

But look what we have done

I know you're loving the view

This is dedicated to you

I'm dedicated to getting rid of limiting beliefs

that tried to drag me under when I wasn't aware

Now I'm doing the work

I'm feeling prepared

For the opportunities that come my way

This is dedicated to you

When I opened my eyes, I took a look at the view

It was an opportunity knocking at my door

I could swear it's been here before

But I never knew it, I was stuck with my
finger on the rewind button

This is dedicated to you if I had to rewind something

This is dedicated to you.

TIP OF THE ICEBERG

They don't see what it took to get to this moment

They didn't see the struggle

Too fascinated with the hustle

The small talk about business

Never took the time out to gain clarity

To see what's underneath the iceberg

They have only seen the tip

It was a trip only to be imagined

It was a trip, a journey only I knew

Stop all the small talk

Doesn't your soul mean more to you

You are a witness to your own demise

Take a look, realize

You had a choice this whole time

To look beyond the tip of the iceberg.

Piere Ingram

LOVING TO WRITE ALONG

This peace at my fingertips

As I write alone in my zone

Sharing a big part of me with the world

It draws them to me

Living my story. I tell you my history

No thoughts or opinions

I tell you

God holds me up

God holds me when I write alone

If I fail, then I did it on my own

Loving to write alone

Why should I give this world my all

when I want to give it all to God?

Loving to write alone is God's message for me

I could feel the peace

I'm loving to write alone.

I'M GOING TO MAKE IT

I'm not a product of my environment

God has offered me way too much to acquire

His hands are out for my soul

So I give it all to the creator of all things

I'm going to make it no matter what
I was destined to achieve

What I already am, catch me if you can

I know what God put me here to do

Just imagine what I'm gonna do

Never to let your true Father down

My true Father handed me the pen to
write myself out of this mess

That carried the message to the people

My true story

To God be the glory

He said His words are the truth

We are the tools in the tool belt

He has equipped us with all we
need to build this kingdom

King, I love you

Appreciate you for putting these things in my heart

No matter what this world tells me.

JUST WRITE

So what? You can't think of anything to write

Just write

Kill the hype of writer's block

We block ourselves from the pen to write

Just write

This craft was designed for us to do

It was meant for a purpose

It moved you

So you throw it away

But it never disappeared

Just write

These problems in your life gave you something to write about

That's the solution in itself

Just write

Piere Ingram

When you felt the lowest in your life

This was a chance to write

To get you in your zone

Even if you're alone

This was your moment to write

Am I right or wrong?

Whatever decisions you made

It gives you something to write about

Just write a poem, a song

PAIN VERSES GAIN

The gain of pain

I gained through the emotions I felt

I dealt with it the best way I knew how

Ow, that hurt

My heart burst through the pain

When I walk through this unknown place

A place of darkness, scarcity, knowing I
came from a place of abundance

Where did this lie creep in from?

How come I wasn't aware?

This pain that came

All I gained was fame

that didn't last long

Just like motivation on a daily basis

I had to grab inspiration

Piere Ingram

From within, He gave me all I needed

Where I would succeed

He put it where I couldn't miss it

Surprisingly, I missed it

Became a misfit of nothing that benefits

But it seemed to fit the pain nicely

Pain and gain much likely.

REFUSE

I refuse to listen to you

No more I say

To these words of decay

We can't play your way anymore

I refuse

Had to put out this fuse

Once was so confused

You don't want to lose

But you seem confused

And a confused mind doesn't buy

The crap you're trying to tell yourself

Stop trying to sell yourself

Your worst enemy is you

I refuse to choose over you,

You lose

I refuse.

Piere Ingram

AT THE DINNER TABLE

As a kid, I used to fall asleep at the dinner table

We had long conversations at that dinner table

What happens at that dinner table
stays at that dinner table

How many family members sit at your dinner table?

I found out who was at that dinner table

I hugged my dad and mom a lot at that dinner table

I learned how to write and do my
math at that same dinner table

God didn't just speak to me, but he spoke
to all of us at that dinner table

What happens at your dinner table?

Did you have fights on that dinner table like I have

Give praise at that dinner table

What if you didn't have a dinner table?

What will be your dinner table?

Praise God for those who had a dinner table and
for those who never experienced a dinner table

HEADED TO THE GOAL

I am the light in the tunnel

I don't have to wait till the end

I'm headed to the goal

My soul is the light that shines bright on cloudy days

Clouds cover the sun

When it breaks it begins before I reach my goal

Headed to the goal

With wings of grace on my back

I fly forward

I'm never going back

I've been ready to run

I've been ready to run this race

Bold enough to face these challenges

I write from my soul

Headed to the goal.

Piere Ingram

STOLEN INNOCENCE

Couldn't fight back a kid who had
his back against the wall

Only if this wall had a phone connected to it

I would have given my parents a call

To tell them what happened

My innocence was stolen, couldn't say a word

Was like I was frozen

At this time, I felt a lot of guilt by adults
telling me what I say didn't matter

That's just part of this heaviness climbing up this ladder

My youth was shattered

Fragments of glass, couldn't recognize my own face

Five years old, a kid that felt like a disgrace

That's just a taste of what happened

Stolen Innocence

HIS CHILDREN

His children are special

He loves his children so much

Why would he let his children die?

Every time a person dies, a child is born

Through death we live, don't be scorned

Plant your seed now

Watch the corn grow for different reasons

In different seasons we are born

We are all different, but similar in ways

We are here to show God's character through us

True love never dies

When are we going to realize this is to all God's children

BLESSINGS IN THE SPIRIT

As we take this walk

Feel the blessings in your heart

Bless everyone who walks with us

Thank you, Lord, for these blessings in the spirit

I hear the whisper

I fall to complete silence

I'm able to dance with you

I enjoyed every moment of these blessings in the spirit

I can hear him speaking to me

I find myself by his whisper

A voice of victory over this sin we win

Then I open my eyes with a gaze of amazement

I love you every way possibly known and
unknown to these blessings in the spirit

As I hear it, we dance

Our love has enhanced

I love you the creator of these blessings in the spirit

RUNNING

They're running

Stop running from who you are

God made you

Stop running from the light

Put up a fight

Everything that we do is good, right?

This is why I write

I am the light

No more running

We have to face what we go through

To come out on the other side of this harsh reality

That some can't face

They can't stand their own face

Stand in place

Wait for God

Piere Ingram

See, we run without him, that's the problem we face

While running this race

But we're running in place

We have it wrong

This is not even a race

This is a marathon

Jesus has passed us the baton

To spread the gospel

Even when these waters are hostile

Speak the truth.

MESSAGE

The other side to me isn't getting the message

But steady he complains about the mess we're in

Stubborn fool

He never seems to listen

Sense a little friction

Got stuck in his position

Forgot all about the mission

But I thought the vision was clear

Obviously couldn't hear

He didn't come to a complete halt

To have empathy for anticipating the
next steps; to take while we review

Now I'm sitting on top of my thoughts
overlooking the view

This message is to you.

Piere Ingram

HIS BURDEN IS LIGHT

Day and night, my heart is heavy

His burden is light

So I dig in deep

I've made a right, a slight turn to
the word I started to read

These are the words that I needed to be

I started to bleed the truth

I began to dig into the roots

I pulled out what was contaminating me

I'm fresh, I left this mess a message to speak

Listen to the words, I'm moving
mountains with every breath

Not the man I used to be, God has changed the game

His burden is light.

IT'S IN YOUR HANDS

Your dreams are in your hands

Stand up if you believe in your dreams

Let your hands do the work

While your mouth brings

them to existence

Destiny turns your dreams into reality

You got this

Your hands were created to do wonderful things

It's in your hands to create

Elevate, Concentrate

Dig deep into your soul

These colors are revealed

through your thoughts spilled out on paper

And these words said to me

Piere Ingram

There's a New World Order, a new version of me

But without this New World Order,
I wouldn't be able to see

what was hidden inside of me

It has to be a disaster to see what
God has mastered in me

The colors are revealed to see these beautiful things

Stand tall for what's to come

It's in your hands

Thy kingdom come.

CRAFT

I see you in my dreams while I'm awake

I see your death happening again
and again in my thoughts

I shall embrace this for it won't take over me

Death is the life I see

These words of God are leading me
to another version of me

My mind sinks in

It confines me to chains of change

He changed the thoughts inside my brain

I embrace the pain to get through

I thought to myself I am through

But he said to me "I am just getting started"

That's what he told me as he works through me

I became something I never imagined inside of my craft

IMPASSION

This is possible

Impassion

He's that passion that never dies in me

A dream in me to speak these words in my mind

I write them down as another round of truth

Faith is the gift God gave me

Maybe if I keep going it will touch the world

With my expression of thought

This isn't an accident

I intentionally set out to live this new life

Impassion

The light that glows who knows it could
change the world starting with me

These words are beauty

At least I won't let that destroy this passion inside

I arrive glowing on stage a human night light

That recites the passion

Every word is a blaze of feelings that
kills the butterflies inside

I am free as a bird

Impassion that stays alive

WHO ARE YOU?

"Who are you?" is what I ask

Why do you wear that mask?

By the way, what's in that flask?

I just don't understand

Maybe if you would let your identity show

Maybe we could grow

I just don't know what to think

But maybe that's not for me to see

How could this be?

I think I'll just let it be

I heard you speak, so I realized
what part of you was in me

Let it be

I see the light now in these dark places

I walk through with faith

My ace, Jesus played the card straight that I was dealt

I felt every scripture in my spirit speaking loudly

It backs me up from the crowd

Now I get down on my knees to bow to the
Most Holy so I can become holy as He is.

YOU CAN DO ANYTHING

Don't wait, just do it

You don't have to prove it to anyone but yourself

You can do anything, just be you

Compete with yourself

I love you like you are

I know you can do this

I can see it in your eyes

Don't disguise yourself,

You're a masterpiece in the making

Look at this beautiful art in the mirror

Your reflection is imperfection

A night light of passion

You may sometimes fight a little friction in your soul

But I tell you, the Lord has made you bold

Dig deep, pull that out of you

You could do anything,

I believe it

You just need to believe it too

There's more to you than you know

But I can see it because you show it

IMPACT ACTION

These actions I performed will leave
an impact in this world

I loved beyond my feeling, so I pushed past the pain

This pain has grown inside to biome my crown of joy

I decided to embrace and grow with the pain

I decided to make impact action

This passion that climbs the ladder to greatness

Look in my eyes of imperfection

I would love you to come walk with me

It's amazing what we can do together in God's love

Time for impact action.

DRIVING FULL SPEED

No More Limits and No Beliefs

No detours

Driving full speed ahead

I see what's in front of me

Are you hungry

I am, get your spoon, fork, get ready to eat with me

Driving Full Speed

I won't leave you alone

Let's do this together

A family that prays together, stays together

But still, you're never alone when you got God

Prepare for the coming of Christ

So let your life speak how you live

Piere Ingram

Let's live for Christ alone

The rest will follow

Don't get swallowed alone

In the belly of the beast

While driving full speed

Don't do it alone, he has his hands out to grab you

If you fall, just please give him a call

You don't have to do this alone while driving full speed.

A MAN'S HEART

A man's heart determines who he is

Lord, please don't allow us to be cold-hearted

Father, may we never be departed from you

You are the wheels that keep our bus moving
at your speed which is good with me

A man's heart guides his life

But you determine where his feet go

Who knows what goes on in some men's hearts

Tell me, do not let me fall for the lives of the other side

Arrive every moment to rescue me

I weep for deliverance

I repent

You are my salvation, save me from myself

For self is what the devil uses to divide me from you

A man's heart.

Piere Ingram

WHAT IF THERE WERE
NO TOMORROW

Let's create the best version of us today

What if there were no tomorrow?

What would you say?

Then tomorrow would just be today.

The Lord determines our steps

Let him usher us into our tomorrow, today

In a way we could never imagine

Let it happen today

We are so wonderfully made

All year round from winter to May

Stay for a while

How do you feel creating your tomorrow today?

Right now, so profound was yesterday

But I found out today that I'm creating my tomorrow

What if yesterday never came?

PRAYED ALL NIGHT

Grace is a wonderful thing

I prayed all night just about grace alone

So thankful for everything that brings light to our lives

I prayed about it all night

When I prayed, it brought what I
thought was gone back to life

Just a little light high on life, connected to a kite

The little boy flew high in the sky

I ain't going to lie

Sometimes it feels like the kite has gone up
while the sky has come down right on me

But I still keep pushing with the sky on my head

I prayed all night instead of worrying
and became a warrior

with my shield to protect me

While I was swinging my sword of salvation

at the enemy, I watch and saw what's going on

I prayed all night.

Piere Ingram

DISCOVER WHAT WAS HIDDEN

What was hidden under the bush

Push to discover what's hidden inside you

It found you before you noticed it

It's been here all along singing sweet songs of praise

Parade to the mighty kingdom inside you

Let's march, hear the drum roll

The sound of feet marching

Hearts hardened

Once was so darkened

The Lord expanded the light

Divided what was good from what was right

Discover the daytime and the
nightlight switch – on and off

My reality started to change with a blink of an eye

Surprise with what God has hidden inside

What a hell of a ride

Riding on a lion with light blue eyes

In the same place where eagles fly

The knights get ready for war

The roar of rage

in battle that rattled the cage

Snakes and riddles

It never explained that they are running
out of time on the shadow clock

Watch for the last hour that devoured all cowards

Stand up for something

Stop falling for anything.

YOU'VE COME TOO FAR

Let's go play 'catch out' in the yard

Son, there's a reason why I push you so hard

Son, grab the ball and mitt for a minute

For you can experience things that I didn't

I admit it, I do push you hard, prodigy

But honestly, I'll be lying to myself if I say
I didn't want to see you go far

Son, I missed so much with my dad

Let's have between us what I never had

One day you'll have a daughter and son too

You will cherish that time too

Because of the gift that you passed on to your little ones

I watched you grow up on the field

So much skill and promise

Everything I've ever wished to be

Seriously, just being honest

Your dreams, I see you and me in it

I admit it, no limits

I see you and me in it

I remember the first field you stepped on

So full of passion

A champion

These moments are priceless

Son, I'm proud

Wow!

Oh, wow! You came too far to quit now.

Piere Ingram

UNLEASH YOUR PURPOSE

There was a lot underneath the surface

that God has to expose in me for his will and purpose

I wouldn't have it any other way

Through his Word, I'm here to stay in it

A mere image of God, The Holy
Ghost speaks through me

We speak in tongues to our father that loves us

He's number one

Like no other sister or brother

Daddy or mother.

He loves us more than we love ourselves

Unleash your purpose in the same place he dwells

Remember the lady at the well

We all fail

Leave it alone, it's about to get backups

Just another reason to pour out the seasons

He's here forever to reign

The one that causes seasons to change

So do your soul the same way he would

Cherish it, don't be ashamed

Forget about embarrassment

Just unleash your purpose.

MAGIC HANDS

Anything I touch turns into a masterpiece

I'm a masterpiece of my master's hands

I handed my life over to the master

That works miracles

Even when the world doesn't understand these miracles

It happens as the world turns

It's your turn to see

what you thought could never be

Let's see what you can do with your magic hands

when you work with your light

I know it

Doesn't it feel right

Am I right to not just live for self
without helping anyone else?

Work with miracles that live underneath your thoughts

Bought something special for you

Aren't you going to ask me what it is

It's not just from me

It's a gift from God.

WHAT'S NEW WITH YOU

Old routines left behind

This new story I started to write for myself

This is for everybody else, while God gets the glory

"What's new with you?" Someone asked.

I looked, I grasped my breath

I said, "Same old routine, but with a brand new story."

I started to embrace the story by the author of many

I understand the words; they fit me perfectly well

Let me tell you what else

What's new? I had a brand new view

of what was being built

I felt it regaining energy

What's new?

Enjoy the ride in the beautiful view.

MY FATHER PICKED ME

I was once a sperm

I made it to the egg

The father picked me

My father picked me to prosper

He healed me

That old me wasn't the real me

He concealed me for the right time

Watch what happens

Applause, the crowd goes

I hear them clap their hands

He's not who he used to be

He's a Godly man

Notebook in the left

Mic in the right hand

While they were sleeping

I was reading the Bible on my nightstand

Stand for something or you'll fall for anything

My father picked me,

MY LOVE LETTER TO GOD

I am never alone when I'm with you

I can't imagine being without you

Being close to my heart

Not just that, you made my heart

How could this world try to tear us apart?

You made that too

I would take note on everything that you do

For me

Show to the world with no scrutiny

I love what you do for me

The person you created

On my path

Brought me out of my past

At last

I can breathe again

With no tubes to use

Your words lit my fuse

Now, I'm not so confused

I was designed by the best

I'll take a rest

Come back at it again

If I fall

You damn right, I'm preaching to y'all about my fall

Because he brought me back, picked me up,
so I can write my love letters to God

WHATS' ON YOUR VISION BOARD

Material things you can't take with
you when you leave here

Never seen a u-haul a funeral

What's on your vision board?

I'm bored from what I've had in the
past on my vision board

I had to change it

Had to live a meaningful life to rearrange it

What's on your vision board?

are there quotes we all heard before?

Are there places you would love to
travel to on your vision board?

I'm bored with what's on my vision board

Show me things on yours that I've never seen before

What's the mission of your vision board?

This is to all the people that don't have a vision board.

Piere Ingram

CREATE YOUR TRUTH

This lie I walked created my truth

The truth exposed the dark

This spark opened my way to the path through my heart

My past is no longer me, not anymore

I pour out my heart

By the tears that fall

After all that, I gave God a call

He answered me on the first ring

I heard this same ring in my ears for years

He was calling me

But why didn't I answer?

Thought I could do this on my own

So foolish of me to think I could do this alone.

Made in the USA
Las Vegas, NV
07 September 2021